SPORTS SUPERSTARS
TRAVIS KELCE

BY THOMAS K. ADAMSON

TORQUE

BELLWETHER MEDIA · MINNEAPOLIS, MN

Torque brims with excitement perfect for thrill-seekers of all kinds. Discover daring survival skills, explore uncharted worlds, and marvel at mighty engines and extreme sports. In *Torque* books, anything can happen. Are you ready?

This edition first published in 2025 by Bellwether Media, Inc.

No part of this publication may be reproduced in whole or in part without written permission of the publisher. For information regarding permission, write to Bellwether Media, Inc., Attention: Permissions Department, 6012 Blue Circle Drive, Minnetonka, MN 55343.

Library of Congress Cataloging-in-Publication Data

LC record for Travis Kelce available at: https://lccn.loc.gov/2024047008

Text copyright © 2025 by Bellwether Media, Inc. TORQUE and associated logos are trademarks and/or registered trademarks of Bellwether Media, Inc.

Editor: Kieran Downs   Designer: Gabriel Hilger

Printed in the United States of America, North Mankato, MN.

TABLE OF CONTENTS

SETTING UP A SUPER WIN 4
WHO IS TRAVIS KELCE? 6
COLLEGE SECOND CHANCE 8
BECOMING A SUPERSTAR 12
KELCE'S FUTURE 20
GLOSSARY 22
TO LEARN MORE 23
INDEX 24

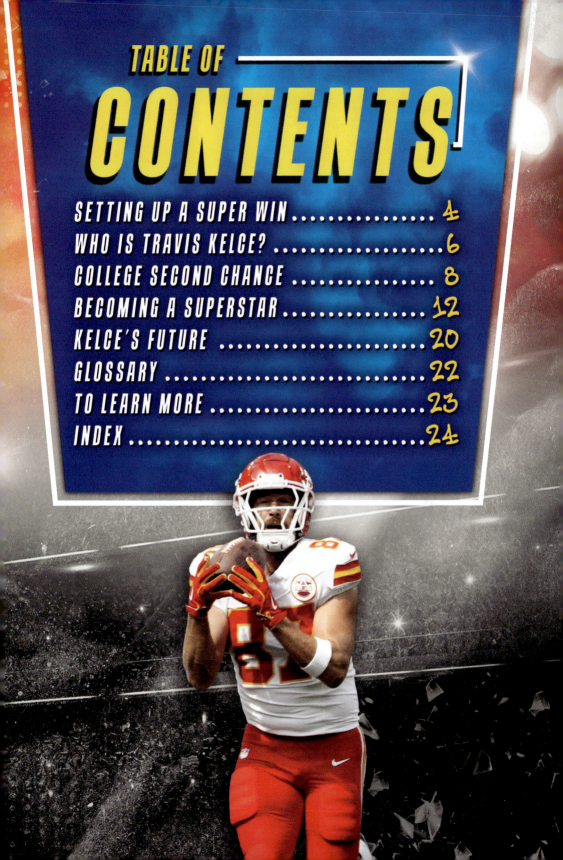

SETTING UP A SUPER WIN

It is near the end of **Super Bowl** 58. The Chiefs are down by 3. **Quarterback** Patrick Mahomes tosses a short pass to Travis Kelce. It looks like he will be tackled for no gain.

But Kelce powers forward. He fights for one more yard. He gets the **first down**! The Chiefs score on their next play and win!

SUPER BOWL 58

TRAVIS KELCE

BACK-TO-BACK

The Chiefs' Super Bowl 58 win was their second Super Bowl win in a row.

WHO IS TRAVIS KELCE?

Travis Kelce is a **tight end** in the **National Football League** (NFL). He is a top pass catcher for the Kansas City Chiefs. He has gained more than 1,000 yards in more seasons than any other NFL tight end.

TRAVIS KELCE

BIRTHDAY October 5, 1989

HOMETOWN Cleveland Heights, Ohio

POSITION tight end

HEIGHT 6 feet 5 inches

DRAFTED Kansas City Chiefs in the 3rd round (63rd overall) of the 2013 NFL Draft

Kelce is well known beyond football. In 2023, he and singer Taylor Swift began dating.

COLLEGE SECOND CHANCE

Kelce played basketball, baseball, and football in high school. In football, he played quarterback. He gained over 2,000 yards in his senior year.

Kelce then went to the University of Cincinnati. His older brother, Jason, also went to school there. Travis was a quarterback at first. He soon switched to tight end.

KELCE AND HIS BROTHER

FAVORITES

PREGAME MEAL
French toast and strawberries

CHRISTMAS MOVIE
A Christmas Story

SODA
Pepsi Wild Cherry

TAYLOR SWIFT SONG
"Blank Space"

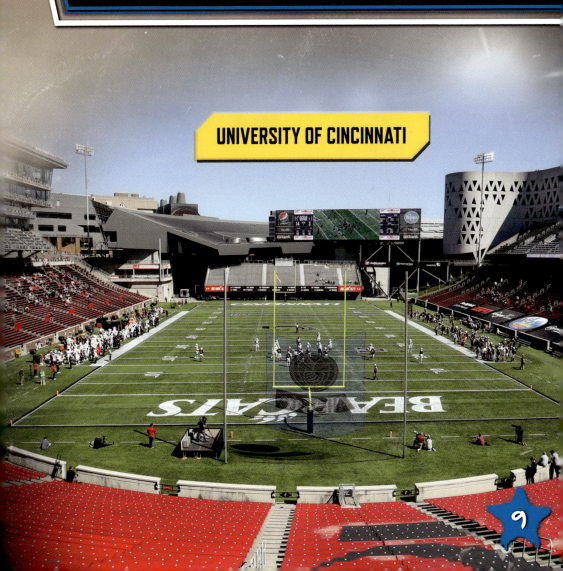

UNIVERSITY OF CINCINNATI

Kelce did not play much at first. In 2010, he was not allowed to play after breaking team rules. Jason talked coaches into giving Travis another chance.

In his senior season in 2012, Kelce set a single-season team record for receiving yards by a tight end. He had 45 catches for 722 yards and 8 **touchdowns**.

BECOMING A SUPERSTAR

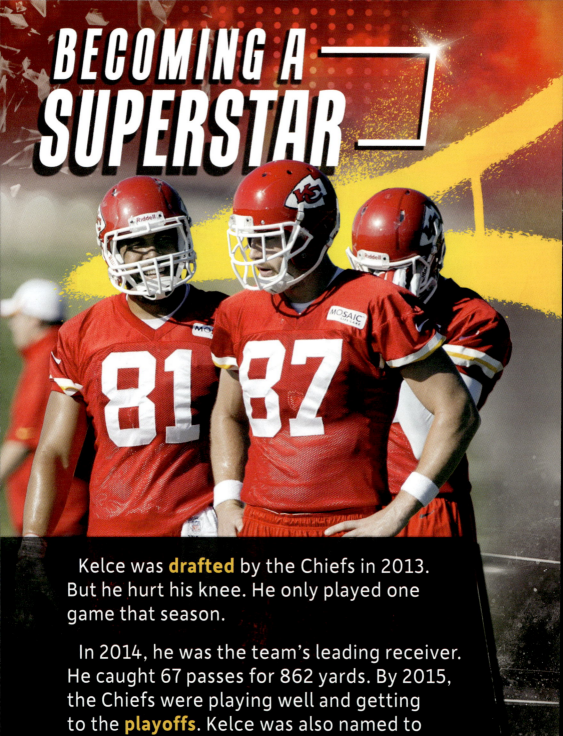

Kelce was **drafted** by the Chiefs in 2013. But he hurt his knee. He only played one game that season.

In 2014, he was the team's leading receiver. He caught 67 passes for 862 yards. By 2015, the Chiefs were playing well and getting to the **playoffs**. Kelce was also named to his first **Pro Bowl**.

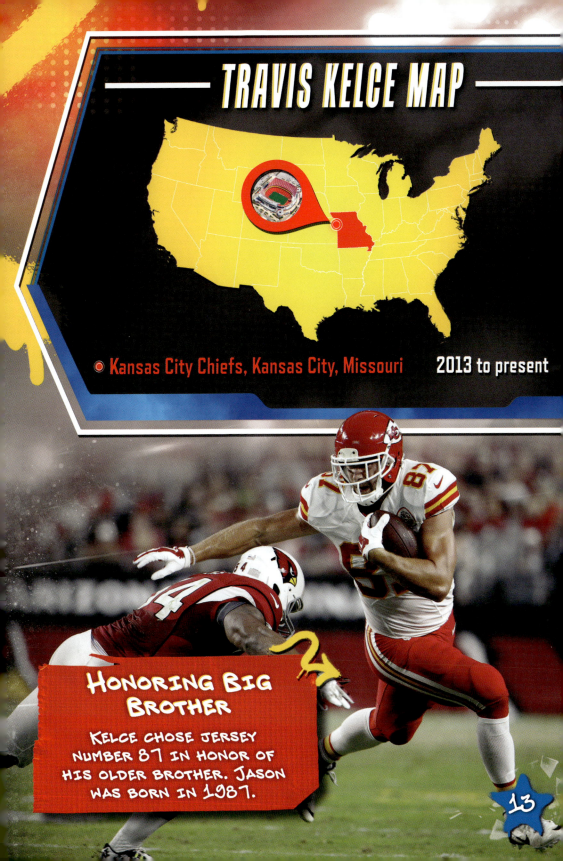

TRAVIS KELCE MAP

Kansas City Chiefs, Kansas City, Missouri — 2013 to present

Honoring Big Brother

Kelce chose jersey number 87 in honor of his older brother. Jason was born in 1987.

In 2016, Kelce led the league in receiving yards among tight ends. He was named a first team **All-Pro** for the first time.

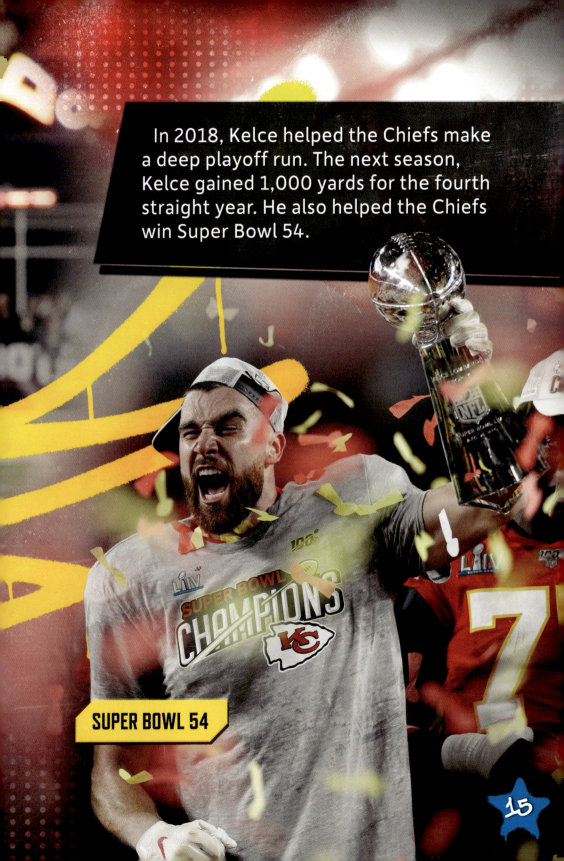

In 2018, Kelce helped the Chiefs make a deep playoff run. The next season, Kelce gained 1,000 yards for the fourth straight year. He also helped the Chiefs win Super Bowl 54.

SUPER BOWL 54

In 2020, Kelce set the receiving record for a tight end with 1,416 yards. His 31 catches for 360 yards in the playoffs led all receivers. The Chiefs again reached the Super Bowl. But they lost.

In the 2021 playoffs, Kelce's 299 yards and three receiving touchdowns led all tight ends. But the Chiefs did not reach the Super Bowl.

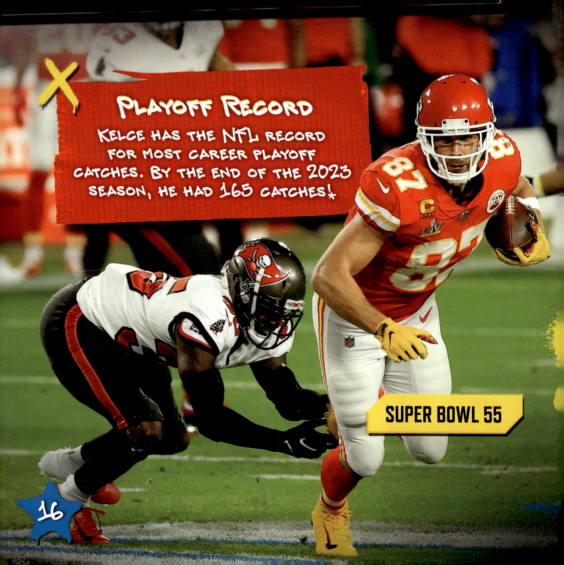

Playoff Record

Kelce has the NFL record for most career playoff catches. By the end of the 2023 season, he had 165 catches!

SUPER BOWL 55

The Chiefs reached the Super Bowl after the 2022 season. This time, Kelce had to play against his brother. The Chiefs beat the Eagles, and Kelce won his second Super Bowl.

The next season, Kelce helped the Chiefs win their second Super Bowl in a row. In April 2024, Kelce signed a new deal. It made him the NFL's highest-paid tight end.

Kelce Bowl

Super Bowl 57 was the first time two brothers were playing on opposing sides in a Super Bowl.

TIMELINE

— 2013 —

Kelce is drafted by the Chiefs

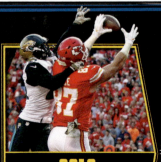

— 2016 —

Kelce leads the NFL in receiving yards among tight ends

SUPER BOWL 58

— 2020 —
The Chiefs win Super Bowl 54

— 2022 —
Kelce gains 1,000 receiving yards for the 7th straight season

— 2024 —
The Chiefs win their second Super Bowl in a row

KELCE'S FUTURE

Kelce started the Eighty-Seven and Running **Foundation**. The group works to help kids in difficult living situations find success.

Kelce is also popular among fans. In 2023, he was named the People's Choice Award **Athlete** of the Year. Kelce also hosts a popular podcast with his brother. He hopes to bring another Super Bowl trophy to Kansas City!

GLOSSARY

All-Pro—an honor for football players who are the best at each position during a season

athlete—a person who is trained in or good at sports that require physical strength and skill

drafted—chosen by a process where professional teams choose high school and college athletes to play for them

first down—a gain of 10 yards in a series of downs, giving the offense another series of downs

foundation—an organization that helps people and communities

National Football League—a professional football league in the United States; the National Football League is often called the NFL.

playoffs—games played after the regular season is over; playoff games determine which teams play in the championship game.

Pro Bowl—a game between the best players in the National Football League

quarterback—a player on offense whose main job is to throw and hand off the ball.

Super Bowl—the annual championship game of the National Football League

tight end—an offensive player who lines up on the end of the offensive line; tight ends both catch passes and block.

touchdowns—scores that occur when a team crosses into their opponent's end zone with the football; a touchdown is worth six points.

TO LEARN MORE

AT THE LIBRARY

Anderson, Josh. *G.O.A.T. Football Tight Ends.* Minneapolis, Minn.: Lerner Publications, 2024.

Morey, Allan. *Patrick Mahomes.* Minneapolis, Minn.: Bellwether Media, 2024.

Stabler, David. *Meet Travis Kelce.* Minneapolis, Minn.: Lerner Publications, 2024.

ON THE WEB

FACTSURFER

Factsurfer.com gives you a safe, fun way to find more information.

1. Go to www.factsurfer.com

2. Enter "Travis Kelce" into the search box and click 🔍.

3. Select your book cover to see a list of related content.

INDEX

All-Pro, 14
awards, 21
catches, 11, 12, 16
childhood, 8
deal, 18
drafted, 12
Eighty-Seven and Running Foundation, 20
favorites, 9
first down, 4
hurt, 12
Kansas City Chiefs, 4, 5, 6, 12, 15, 16, 18, 21
Kelce, Jason, 8, 10, 13, 18, 21
map, 13
National Football League, 6, 16, 18
playoffs, 12, 15, 16, 17
podcast, 21
Pro Bowl, 12
profile, 7
quarterback, 4, 8
records, 6, 11, 16, 18
Super Bowl, 4, 5, 15, 16, 18, 19, 21
Swift, Taylor, 7
tight end, 6, 8, 11, 14, 16, 18
timeline, 18–19
touchdowns, 11, 16
trophy shelf, 17
University of Cincinnati, 8, 9, 10, 11
yards, 4, 6, 8, 11, 12, 14, 15, 16

The images in this book are reproduced through the courtesy of: Ryan Kang/ AP Images, cover; Ringo Chiu, p. 3; Michael Owens/ Contributor/ Getty Images, p. 4; Steph Chambers/ Staff/ Getty Images, p. 5; Kansas City Chiefs/ AP Images, p. 6; Paul Spinelli/ AP Images, p. 7 (Travis Kelce); Ed Zurga/ AP Images, p. 8; Ian Johnson/ Icon Sportswire/ AP Images, p. 9 (University of Cincinnati); Elena Veselova, p. 9 (French toast and strawberries); Everett Collection, Inc./ Alamy, p. 9 (*A Christmas Story*); Steve Cukrov, p. 9 (Pepsi Wild Cherry); Kevin Mazur/ TAS24/ Contributor/ Getty Images, p. 9 (Taylor Swift); Mel Evans/ AP Images, p. 10; Andy Lyons/ Staff/ Getty Images, p. 11; Kansas City Star/ Contributor/ Getty Images, p. 12; Greg Trott/ AP Images, p. 13; Paparacy, p. 13 (Kansas City Chiefs stadium); Steven Senne/ AP Images, p. 14; Scott Boehm/ AP Images, p. 15; Mike Ehrmann/ Staff/ Getty Images, p. 16; Margaret Bowles/ AP Images, p. 17; Ben Liebenberg/ AP Images, p. 18 (Kelce brothers); Raffaele1 | Dreamstime.com; p. 18 (Chiefs logo); Tim Umphrey/ AP Images, p. 18 (2016); Michael Owens/ Contributor/ Getty Images, p. 19 (Super Bowl 58); Ryan Kang/ AP Images, p. 19 (2020); David Eulitt/ Contributor/ Getty Images, p. 20; ZUMA Press, Inc.; Alamy, p. 21; Cal Sport Media/ Alamy, p. 23.